SPORTS AND GAMES THE INDIANS GAVE US

Other books by
Alex Whitney

STIFF EARS
ONCE A BRIGHT RED TIGER
VOICES IN THE WIND

SPORTS & GAMES

THE INDIANS GAVE US

 With step-by-step instructions for
making Indian gaming equipment

ALEX WHITNEY

drawings and diagrams by Marie and Nils Ostberg

DAVID McKAY COMPANY, INC. New York

SPORTS AND GAMES THE INDIANS GAVE US

Library of Congress Cataloging in Publication Data

Whitney, Alex.
Sports & games the Indians gave us.

Bibliography: p.
Includes index.
1. Indians of North America—Games—Juvenile literature.
I. Ostberg, Marie. II. Ostberg, Nils. III. Title.
E98.G2W47   796   76-44350
ISBN 0-679-20391-5

Designed by Marie and Nils Ostberg

10 9 8 7 6 5 4 3 2 1

MANUFACTURED IN THE UNITED STATES OF AMERICA

CONTENTS

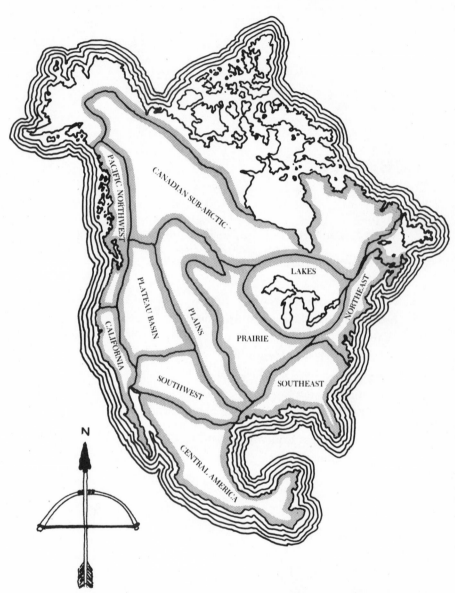

(Some tribes are extinct; some still live in the area
in which they originally settled;
others have been forced to move elsewhere.)

Major Indian Tribes
of the
North American Continent

PACIFIC NORTHWEST
Bellabella
Bellacoola
Chinook
Haida
Klamath
Kwakiutl
Makah
Nootka
Quileute
Quinault
Salish
Tlinglit
Tsimshian

CALIFORNIA
Chumash
Costano
Hupa
Karok
Maidu
Mission
Miwok
Modoc
Pomo
Salinan
Shasta
Wintun
Yokuts

Yurok

SOUTHWEST
Acoma
Apache
Arizona Papago
Chiricahua Apache
Havasupai
Hopi
Maricopa
Navajo
Pima
Pueblo
Walapai
Yavapai
Yuma
Zuni

PLATEAU-BASIN
Bannock
Cayuse
Flathead
Gosiute
Kutenai
Mono
Nez Percé
Paiute
Panamint
Paviotso
Piegan
Shoshoni

Shuswap
Thompson
Ute
Washo
Yakima

PLAINS
Arapaho
Assinboin
Blackfoot
Cheyenne
Comanche
Crow
Gros Ventre
Kiowa
Sioux
Teton Sioux

PRAIRIE
Arikara
Dakota
Hidatsa
Illinois
Ioway
Kansas
Mandan
Miami
Missouri
Omaha
Osage
Oto
Pawnee
Ponca
Santee
Shawnee

Wichita
Yankton

LAKES
Chippewa
Fox
Kickapoo
Menomini
Ottawa
Pottawatomi
Sauk
Winnebago

SOUTHEAST
Alabamu
Apalachee
Atakapa
Biloxi
Caddo
Calusa
Catawba
Cherokee
Chickahominy
Chickasaw
Chitimacha
Choctaw
Creek
Koasati
Natchez
Powhatan
Quapaw
Seminole
Timucua
Tuscarora

NORTHEAST

Abnaki
Algonkian
Beothuk
Conestoga
Delaware
Erie
Iroquois
Leni-Lenape
Mohican
Malecite
Massachuset
Micmac
Nanticoke
Narragansett
Passamaquoddy
Pennacook
Penobscot
Pequot
Powhaton
Shinnecock

CANADIAN SUB-ARCTIC

Algonkian
Beaver
Carrier
Chipewyan
Cree
Dogrib
Hare
Ingalik
Kaska
Khotana

Kutchin
Montagnais
Nahane
Naskapi
Sarsi
Satudene
Sekani
Slave
Tahaina
Yellow Knife

CENTRAL AMERICA

Aztec
Chorotega
Coahuntec
Concho
Huatec
Lacandones
Lagunero
Lenca
Maya
Mixtec
Mosquita
Olmec
Otomi
Papago
Quiché
Seri
Tarahumara
Tarascan
Toltec
Yaqui
Zapotec

"Out of childhood into manhood
Now had grown my Hiawatha,
Skilled in all the craft of hunters,
Learned in all the lore of old men,
In all youthful sports and pastimes. . . .

Swift of foot was Hiawatha;
He could shoot an arrow from him,
And run forward with such fleetness,
That the arrow fell behind him!"

—from *The Song of Hiawatha,*
    by Henry Wadsworth Longfellow

SPORTS AND GAMES
THE INDIANS GAVE US

OUR AMERICAN INDIAN HERITAGE

An Indian brave streaking across the ice, shuttling a puck before him with a curved stick, was a familiar sight to many of North America's earliest inhabitants. The name of their game was *shinny,* the forerunner of both field and ice hockey. It was a favorite sport of almost every tribe from Canada to the Mexican border, and from the Pacific to the Atlantic coasts.

Hockey was only one of many sports and games we inherited from the Indians. Hundreds of centuries before Columbus set sail on his historic voyage, Indian athletes were playing their versions of sports we enjoy today: baseball, football, basketball, soccer, wrestling, bowling, and sky-diving—to name just a few.

Some Indian sports were created for instructive and practical purposes, rather than for recreation and amusement. As part of their training, young would-be warriors ran relay races nearly every evening. In Mexico, Aztec and Toltec hunters and warriors practiced their marksmanship in *Atl-Atl* (spear-throwing) contests. And during this same period in history, lacrosse, or "little-brother-of-war," was developed as a battle-training exercise for a great number of North American tribes.

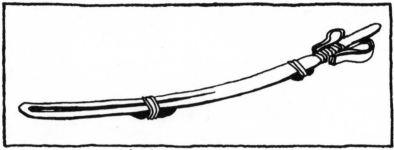

an Atl-Atl *(spear-throwing board)*

Certain sports were regarded as serious matters by the Indians, since their possessions and the honor of their villages were often at stake. In Yucatan and Guatemala, for example, it was not uncommon for the people in the viewing stands to vanish whenever a team scored at *Pok-to-Pok*, a combination of soccer and basketball originated by the ancient Maya; spectators were supposed to donate their jewelry to the winning players.

But the majority of Indian sports and games did not feature material rewards nor the practice of skills in the hunt and on the warpath. Tribes throughout the North American continent encouraged sports requiring widespread participation by both sexes of all ages. Almost every able-bodied person played kickball, from grandmothers and grandfathers to youngsters barely out of the toddling stage. Juggling, bowling, darts, games of chance, guessing games, and tug-of-war contests were among the other pastimes shared by children and adults.

Children's games have remained almost unchanged over the centuries. Then, as now, Indian boys and girls played blindman's buff, tag, follow-the-leader, prisoner's base, crack-the-whip, and hide-and-seek. They also amused themselves with their versions of hopscotch, marbles, and jack-straws, using whatever materials were on hand: seeds, bones, shells, stones, grasses, wood, feathers, and vegetables.

No two American tribes were exactly alike. Each tribe's culture and way of life was closely linked to the climate and terrain in which the tribe lived. Yet anthropologists and archaeologists have discovered that the sports and games of tribes who lived throughout North America were remarkably similar. The Nahane Indians of the Canadian sub-Arctic region used the same type of equipment and had the same rules for one of their acrobatic sports as did the Toltec tribes who lived half a hemisphere away in Mexico. The Hopi, whose homeland lay in northeastern Arizona, vied with one another in a game called "snakes." The object of the game was to see which competitor could slide a stick farthest on the ground. "Snow-snake" contests were held in winter by the Iroquois tribes of the Northeast, who slid their sticks on ice or snow.

We are indebted to the American Indians for their countless contributions to our present-day knowledge of architecture, engineering, surgery, medicine, astronomy, agriculture, mathematics, and arts and crafts. More than half the global population owes its subsistence to corn, beans, and potatoes—all cultivated and introduced by the Indians. And our Indian benefactors are responsible for another important part of our heritage—the sports and games they gave us.

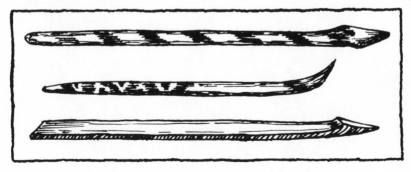

BALL GAMES

More Indian games featured balls than any other athletic equipment. Tribes who lived north of the gulf of Mexico made balls out of deerskin or buffalo hide, stuffing them with a wide variety of materials—corn husks, cedar bark, moss, grass, feathers, sand, pebbles, seeds, and animal or human hair. Most Central American tribes made rubber balls from the milky sap of certain tropical plants. And nearly every tribe knew how to fashion balls out of animals' bladders, which they cleaned, blew up with air, and then tied.

Indian ball games fell into four major categories: those played with a netted racket; shinny games, in which the ball was struck with a bat or a curved club; double-ball games, played with two or more balls tied together and tossed with a stick; and ball-race games, in which a ball was batted, kicked, or propelled by the elbow, knee, or hip.

LACROSSE

The most popular ball game of the North American Indians— from Hudson Bay to the Gulf of Mexico, and from the Atlantic coast to the Plains—was *Tokonhon,* or "little-brother-of-war." This free-for-all sport, with few fixed rules, was later adopted by the French settlers and renamed lacrosse. The original Indian version was usually a contest between two intertribal teams, and each team numbered from ten to several hundred players. Playing fields ranged in size from two hundred yards to over a mile in length. At each end of the field the goals were marked by two upright poles. Each player was equipped with a racket consisting of a smooth, hardwood stick, bent at one end into a semi-hoop that formed a small pocket crisscrossed with rawhide thongs. Southeastern tribes preferred to use two rackets, but other tribes used only one.

At the start of a game, two teams lined up opposite each other in the center of a field. Then a stuffed deerskin ball (approximately three inches in diameter) was tossed between the teams, and the players tried to catch it in the pockets of their rackets. The object of the game was to hurl, carry, or kick the ball between the opposing team's goal posts, but the long-range aim was to test a young man's endurance and potential valor on the battlefield.

SHINNY

Another ball game, played by every North American tribe, was shinny °, the ancestor of both field and ice hockey. Preparations for an intertribal match began several months in advance. During this period, the players held to a rigid diet and trained daily for the event.

When shinny was played on a field, a stuffed deerskin ball was kicked or batted with a four-foot wooden stick, similar in shape to a modern hockey stick. Playing fields were roughly four hundred yards long, with goal posts at either end. Each team numbered from ten to fifty players. The game began when a referee, called a "watcher," placed the ball in the center of the playing field or tossed it in the air. When he gave a signal, all the players—with the exception of those guarding their respective goals—raced toward the ball, which they tried to bat or kick between their rivals' goal posts. The first team to score seven goals won the game.

Indian men often played shinny from mid-morning to late afternoon, without a break. During their almost superhuman struggles for the ball, they pushed, pulled, butted, and battered each other. Broken bones were common occurrences.

Needless to say, shinny was another war-training exercise for Indian braves. But women and girls played a modified version of the sport, with rules that eliminated much of the violence that marked the men's game.

DOUBLE-BALL

Double-ball, regarded as strictly a woman's sport, was even faster and more difficult than shinny, although far less rigorous. The game was played with two stuffed deerskin balls (or rounded chunks of wood) and a stick, tapered and slightly curved at the

° *also see Winter Sports and Games*

striking end. The balls, sometimes weighted with sand or pebbles, were attached to each end of a one-foot-long rawhide cord. Double-ball goals were composed of two single posts set four hundred yards apart. Any number could play, but each team usually consisted of ten to twelve women.

As soon as a watcher tossed the double-ball between the teams, each player tried to catch the cord with her stick and pass it along to a teammate toward the opponents' goal post. Or the double-ball could be hurled down the length of the field. Each time a team member wrapped the cord and balls around her rivals' goal post, she scored a point for her side. The first team to score five points won the game.

Little Indian girls began learning double-ball by the time they were four years old. They were taught to play the game with small sticks, notched to make it easier for them to catch and carry the cord attached to the balls.

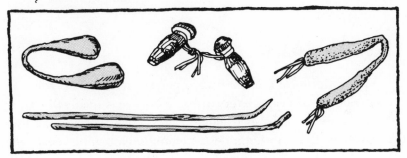

FOOT-CATCH

Tribeswomen were also adept at a form of catch, a game which was much harder than it looked. Each contestant balanced a small buckskin ball on top of her foot and kicked the ball upward into the air. When it came down, she caught it on her foot. The player able to repeat this accomplishment the greatest number of times was the winner.

DODGE-BALL

Baseball may well have its roots in *Onagon,* or dodge-ball, a game originated by the Pawnee, Mandan, and other Prairie tribesmen. One player was selected as the batter, and eight players were the fielders. The batter stood within a four-foot circle, which was outlined with small stones imbedded in the ground. He opened the game by tossing a moss-filled, rawhide ball into the air. His object was to bat it with a four-foot stick of hardwood beyond the reach of the fielders. If a fielder caught it in mid-air, he remained in the spot where he caught the ball and threw it at the batter, who was supposed to stay within the circle. If the batter was unable to dodge the ball, he became a fielder. The player who hit him became the batter.

KICK-BALL

Various forms of kick-ball were played by the men, women, and children of nearly every tribe. Two teams, generally with twelve runners each, sped along a cross-country course of five hundred yards up to ten miles or more. Each team had its own wooden ball, about the size of a croquet ball, often covered with gum or pitch. The players on each team took turns kicking their ball to the end of the course and back. The winning team, of course, was the first to kick the ball back to the starting point.

The men's version of the game was somewhat reminiscent of modern football, since it was permissable to block and tackle one's rivals. But no matter how the game was played, the participants usually suffered from sore toes. More often than not, the ball landed in rocky hollows or among clumps of thorny bushes and had to be kicked out of the "rough" and back on the course as quickly as possible.

JUGGLING

According to anthropologists, one of the oldest ball contests, held by members of all the North American Indian tribes, was the juggling of two or more balls or other objects. Most of the California and northwestern tribes preferred to juggle wooden sticks or small gourds. Northeastern Indians juggled balls made of wood, stone, or stuffed deerhide. Aztec jugglers at Emperor Montezuma's court in Mexico performed with solid rubber balls, and the Chinook Indians of Washington and Oregon were able to rotate as many as seven pebbles in the air at the same time.

BOWLING

A great number of North American tribes held various kinds of bowling tournaments. At one Cherokee mound-site in Georgia, archaeologists uncovered several twenty-foot-long bowling alleys constructed of hardened clay.

Indians of the Southwest rolled wooden balls at upright corncob targets. The Cherokee and their southeastern neighbors pitched stone balls at clay objects shaped like the Indian clubs we use today in tenpins and other bowling games.

The Caddo Indians of Louisiana and Arkansas had another type of bowling contest. They drew a line on the ground with a stick, dividing an area thirty feet wide by seventy feet long into two equal-sized courts. Six Indian clubs, molded of clay, were placed at one end of each court. Each team occupied its own court and had its own seed-filled, deerskin ball—about the size of a modern basketball. One team member opened the game by rolling a ball into the competing players' court in an attempt to knock over their clay targets. If one was knocked down, it was left so, and the next player took over. The first team to topple all of their opponents' clubs won the round.

11

BALL COURT GAMES

Every major Maya city in Mexico and Guatemala contained a ball court where *Pok-to-Pok* was played. The same sport was popular with the Indians of southern Arizona and the Aztec, Toltec, and other Central American tribes, who called it *Tlachtli*.

Each ball court was about fifty feet wide and slightly longer than a modern football field. It was flanked on two sides by high, stone walls. Small temples at either end served as viewing stands for the priests and nobility. Two massive stone rings, usually carved with feathered serpents, were set vertically on each wall, twenty-four feet above the ground.

The game combined the features of both basketball and soccer. Using elbows, knees, and hips—but not hands—the five players on each side attempted to drive a solid rubber ball through an eighteen-inch hole in their opponents' ring. Whenever a player accomplished this rare and exciting feat, the spectators hastily departed, since custom dictated that the scorer was entitled to their jewelry—if he could catch the reluctant donors.

TRAP-BALL

The Yaqui tribes of northern Mexico played a game in which each contestant used an entangling device of four balls carved out of wood. The balls were connected by four four-foot-long cords to a main cord of eight feet. When a player threw it accurately, it temporarily—but effectively—tied up a man's arms or legs.

Trap-ball playing areas were approximately one hundred yards wide by two hundred yards long, divided in the center by a taut cord tied to two posts on each side of the field. Before the game began, the seven players on each team lined up at the

farthest end of their respective sides of the field. When a watcher gave the starting signal, each player ran toward the center of the field, simultaneously hurling his trap-ball at an onrushing opponent. The first competitor to cross the center line, without becoming ensnared by a rival's trap-ball, scored a point for his team. The first team to acquire five points won the contest.

3

ACROBATIC AND
ENDURANCE CONTESTS

A great number of tribes were often forced to migrate in pursuit of drinking water and food supplies: fish or game; and the nuts, berries, and plants which supplemented their diet. But wherever they settled—in warm, temperate, or sub-Arctic zones—their lifestyles, with very few exceptions, were rugged at best. And although their acrobatic and endurance sports (with the exception of certain kinds of tug-of-war) were developed purely for recreational purposes, they reflected the importance the tribes placed on maintaining physical fitness.

TOSSING CONTESTS

Tossing was an Indian acrobatic sport, reminiscent of modern-day trampoline contests. The Nahane Indians of the sub-Arctic used a walrus hide, which they placed flat on the ground. As soon as a tribesman stood in the center of the skin, a group of thirty or more participants jerked the skin upward, throwing the person high in the air. A contestant might be tossed as high as twenty feet. If he managed to land on his feet on the stretched skin, he was again tossed upward. But if he missed, he exchanged places with one of the tossers.

The ancient Toltec tribes of Mexico competed in a similar contest, but they used a woven blanket instead of an animal hide.

The Makah Indians of northern Washington held "dancing-in-air" competitions. From four whale-jaw tripods, a walrus hide was stretched by ropes about five feet above the ground. Fifty or more tribesmen clutched special rope handgrips on the hide's edge, and together they tossed a player at least twenty feet high. A skilled contestant was able to keep his feet dancing in the air for several moments before he landed on the ground.

Two teams of the Blackfoot tribe played a tossing game in which a man from one side stood on a buffalo robe held by the members of the other side. The robe-tossing team then tried to throw him as high as possible, hoping he would give a signal indicating he had been tossed enough. If the tossers were unable to make him do this, the opposing team won.

The Navajo and other tribes of the Southwest competed in a dangerous acrobatic sport. Two braided moose-skin thongs were stretched diagonally between four trees, growing thirty feet apart in the shape of a square. The thongs formed an X, approximately twenty feet above the ground. Where they intersected, a small wooden platform was attached. When a player stood on the platform and jumped up and down on it, the cord's elasticity threw him higher, until he was propelled more than ten feet above the platform. The higher he bounced, the more difficult it became to keep his balance. The object was to see who could complete the greatest number of jumps before falling to the ground far below.

STILT-RACING

Ancient Maya hieroglyphs in Yucatan and Guatemala depict warriors racing on stilts. In Arizona, New Mexico, Oklahoma, and Wyoming, archaeologists have found Indian stilts made of hardwood, with forked notches for the feet. Early Spanish explorers have recorded eye-witness accounts of Indian stilt races, held on long, arduous courses, which required the participants to take broadjumps on their stilts over trenches, logs, and other obstacles.

POLE-FLYING

The Otomi Indians of Mexico practiced a death-defying type of acrobatic sport, featuring some of the aspects of modern sky-diving. Four tribesmen climbed up a seventy-foot pole, at the top of which was a moveable, thimble-like cylinder in the form of a hollowed-out log. The men, fastened to ropes wound around and around the cylinder, braced their feet against the pole and hurled themselves backward into space. As they did so, the ropes began to unwind—slowly at first, then faster and faster—and the four acrobats swung in increasingly wider circles until they landed on the ground. This dizzying sport still survives in remote hamlets northeast of Mexico City.

HORSEBACK-TILTING

Although fossil bones prove there were horses in North America many thousands of years ago, the animals were slightly smaller than the Arabian stock brought to the western plains by the Spanish during the sixteenth century. When a number of the Spaniards' mounts escaped, they bred and multiplied in the lush grasslands of the region. The Ute, Apache, Arapaho, Comanche, and Kiowa tribesmen were among the first to catch and tame the wild herds, and nowhere in the world did more expert horsemen develop.

Indians usually rode bareback. Their bridles were thongs looped around the horses' lower jaws. Horses provided the tribes with greater speed for hunting, raiding, and warfare, and with a sport not unlike the tilting tournaments popular in medieval Europe.

Two teams, each numbering at least twenty horses and twenty riders, rode at full gallop toward each other. Each member wore a colored, team-identifying headband, and carried a three-foot pole, which was padded at one end. With their bodies low to the horses' withers, the riders attempted to unseat their opponents by prodding or pushing them with the padded ends of their poles. Those who were dismounted were out of the game, which continued until all the members of one team had been unseated. An exceptionally agile player often managed to avoid an opponent's pole by slipping to the side of his galloping horse and placing his head beneath the animal's neck.

HAWK-FIGHTING

The Cherokee tribes were adept at a contest in which two braves crouched on the ground and faced each other. Then each brought his knees together under his chin and grasped his legs with his arms. The match began when a non-player placed a four-foot tree limb under each player's knees and over his arms. Then they approached each other as best they could. The first man who succeeded in tipping over the other, without dislodging his own tree limb, was acclaimed the winner.

BREATH-HOLDING CONTESTS

An unusual kind of endurance contest, held by the Nootka Indians of Vancouver, was a test of lung capacity. Twelve players broke off alternate branches on a long tree limb. Then each member of the group in turn held the limb and touched one branch after another, each time saying *"pina,"* without taking a breath. The player who could go farthest down the limb, before having to inhale, won the game.

The Klamath Indians of southern Oregon had a similar game. The young men of the tribe ran forward, crying *"wo yi,"* without taking a breath. When each person could no longer do so, he halted. The contestant who could run the farthest won.

TUG-OF-WAR CONTESTS

Each tribe had its own favorite version of this endurance sport °, which was sometimes used as a method of settling disputes over hunting or fishing boundaries and other tribal or intertribal disagreements.

Tribes of the Northwest and Far North held a contest between two teams, each consisting of twenty or more men. The two leaders of each team locked hands, and their teammates lined up behind them, each grasping his arms around the person in front of him. The first team to pull the other side across a dividing line won the game.

Iroquois tribeswomen were fond of a triangular tug-of-war, in which three players competed at one time. They first tied the ends of a six-foot-long rawhide cord. Then they spread themselves in a triangular formation, holding the cord taut. A nonplayer placed a stone in front of each corner of the triangle, well out of the reach of each contestant. When a signal was given, each tribeswoman tried to pick up the stone nearest her, without

° *also see Water Sports and Winter Sports and Games*

letting go of the cord. The first player to pick up a stone won the contest.

The Hopi and Apache tribes reversed the usual tug-of-war procedure and played push-of-war, a contest in which they tried to shove their opponents backward.

In 1906, two factions in the Hopi village of Oraibi decided to settle an argument over a tribal policy by a push-of-war. It was agreed beforehand that the losers would leave Oraibi and settle elsewhere. In the ensuing contest, one side pushed the other back across a line drawn on the ground. The defeated team members and their families departed and founded the village of Hotevilla several miles away.

WRESTLING

North American Indians held wrestling matches all year round, both indoors and outdoors. The tournaments began with two wrestlers facing each other, feet spread apart. Then each wrestler placed one hand over the back of the other's neck, at the same time grasping his opponent's arm near the elbow.

At the start of a bout, it was not uncommon for the two smallest boys of a tribe to grapple with each other. The winner then took on the next largest boy, who tried to attack his competitor before that one could catch his breath. Thus the contest proceeded, without a pause, until the largest and strongest tribesmen confronted each other. An expert wrestler might have thrown four or five men to the ground before he in turn was bested by the overall champion.

The rules for many of the southwestern Indians' wrestling matches were catch-as-catch-can, allowing the participants to trip one another and to drag each other around by the hair. The winner was the wrestler who succeeded in forcing his opponent's two shoulders to touch the ground simultaneously. In order to get a better grip on each other, the two contenders often rubbed their bodies with tallow, which they then dusted with powdered clay or sand.

The sport we call Indian wrestling was familiar to every North American tribe. In one version, two wrestlers lay side by side on their backs, in reversed positions. Then they locked their near arms and raised and locked their corresponding legs in an attempt to force each other's leg down and to turn the other wrestler on his face.

In another variation of the sport, two contenders stood face to face, gripped each other's right hand, and set the outsides of their right feet tightly against one another's. Then each tried to force the other off balance.

In the third version of Indian wrestling, two competitors sat face to face at either side of a flat-topped rock or log section and gripped right hands. Then each placed his right elbow against his adversary's elbow on the rock or log. The wrestler who forced his opponent's arm down, without moving his own elbow, became the winner.

DEXTERITY AND MARKSMANSHIP GAMES

Every North American tribe had contests in which dexterity determined the outcome. They also held target-shooting games, featuring such weapons as spears, blow-guns, darts, slingshots, and bows and arrows.

BOW-AND-ARROW CONTESTS

For many thousands of centuries, the Indians' most important weapons were their bows and arrows. Stone arrowheads have been found embedded in the bones of giant bison and other extinct animals of the pre-glacial era.

Bows were made from many kinds of hardwoods as well as from bone and horn. Most were made of wood and wrapped with animal sinew. Some were constructed with layers of wood that were glued and lashed together with sinew. Still others were carved from solid lengths of wood.

Arrows were slender, wooden shafts, usually feathered at one end. At the other end, a pointed arrowhead, made out of rock, bone, antlers, or copper, was lashed securely to the shaft.

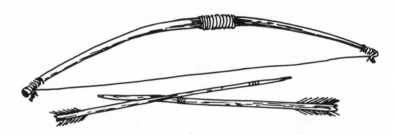

Accuracy, distance, and timing were the prime factors of most Indian archery contests. In one game, men competed to see how many rapidly fired arrows they could keep aloft simultaneously. Southwestern and northern Mexican tribesmen tested their skill by shooting arrows through small holes cut in yucca plants. California Indians practiced shooting at an arrow or a sapling branch stuck upright in the ground.

The Blackfoot tribes competed in walking-archery contests. When one bowman shot an arrow ahead of him into the ground, his opponents used it as a target. From the location of the first arrow, a second arrow was shot ahead. Thus the game continued until all the arrows in the players' quivers had been used. The contestant with the highest score was awarded all the arrows that had been shot.

The Pawnee tribes of the Plains shot arrows fifty yards ahead in such a way that they fell flat on the ground. The other players took turns trying to shoot their arrows so they would fall directly across the first arrows. The Pawnee Indians also wrapped grass around oval pieces of bark, which they tossed in the air. Each archer tried to hit the bundles before they fell to the ground.

Indian boys learned to become good marksmen as soon as they were big enough to handle miniature bows and small, blunt

arrows. By the time they reached the age of seven or eight, they were given arrows with pointed tips and taught how to shoot at moving targets and how to hunt small game, such as birds and rabbits. Young Indians of the Plains divided themselves into two armies and took part in make-believe battles in which they shot arrows tipped with padded deerhide. A more difficult bow-and-arrow game was played by Zuni youths, who shot at corncobs placed upright on the ground in a V formation.

ATL-ATL CONTESTS

The Aztec, Toltec, Olmec, and Zapotec tribes of Central America held spear-throwing contests, using *atl-atls*, or throwing boards. Each contestant's spear was a long shaft with a sharp head of bone, flint, or metal. This he laid along his atl-atl, a narrow, wooden trough. He then grasped the nearer end with his hand, and with this extension of his arm he was able to give a greater propulsive force to his spear. Polished and decorated stones, called "banners," about five inches long and weighing almost a pound, were often secured to the atl-atl in order to give the board the proper balance.

RING-AND-PIN GAMES

Games using rings and pins were popular with all Indian women, men, and children. Although the equipment varied from tribe to tribe, it generally consisted of a series of rings, or a single target, attached to a pin by a short thong. The Prairie tribes used a single hide ring; Northwestern Indians used strings of hollow deer toebones or salmon bones; Southwestern tribes preferred gourd rinds; and the Northeastern and Southeastern Indians used balls of moose hair or oval targets woven of grass. Most of the pins were pointed pieces of bone or wood.

Two players usually competed at one time, and the object was to thrust a pin through a single target or a graduated series of rings. Tossing up a string of rings, attached to a short cord, and impaling one or more of them on a pointed stick was much more difficult than it appeared. Of course, single targets were much easier to spear.

The more rings a contestant was able to spear, the more points he scored. But the end of the thong near the target usually had several holes in it, and a player who successfully thrust his pin through one or more of the holes raised his score even higher.

In the Hopi version of the game, a ring of wrapped corn husks was placed flat on the ground eight feet away from two competitors. Each competitor had two feathered darts which he then tried to hurl through the center of the ring.

Still another ring-and-pin contest was held by the Mohican tribesmen of the Northeast, who attempted to sail wooden darts through a twirling ring suspended from the ceiling of their communal longhouse.

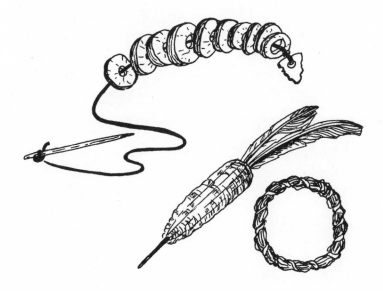

HOOP-AND-POLE GAMES

Of all the Indians' games of dexterity, the most widely played was hoop-and-pole, a contest similar to chunkey.° Many tribes had legends describing how the hoop-and-pole game was acquired from their gods. Other tribes had special hoop-and-pole ceremonies and songs. But for most Indians a hoop-and-pole game was the major sporting event for an entire village, and each village had hoop-and-pole playing fields, enclosed with sloping sides for avid spectators.

The gaming implements differed in each region, but they generally consisted of a circular hoop, ranging from eight inches to two feet in diameter, and pointed wooden poles about eight feet long.

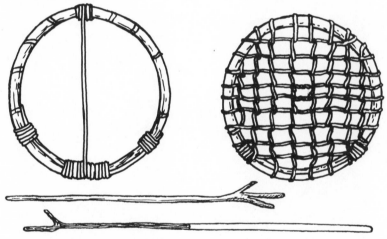

The kind of hoop most commonly used was made of a stripped sapling, tied at either end with animal sinew or rawhide thongs. Lake tribes made hoops of elm bark, while Southwestern Indians wrapped bark hoops with yucca fiber or corn husks. Prairie Indians often wrapped their wooden hoops with beads, and some

° *also see Winter Sports and Games*

tribes carved their hoops out of stone. Most of the hoops were webbed with a network of rawhide thongs, but some had only a single cord across the hoop's center.

Two tribesmen competed in the hoop-and-pole game. Each had his own pole and shared a single hoop with his opponent. One of the players started the contest by rolling the hoop down the course of a playing field. Both players then slid their poles along the ground after it. A player's ultimate aim was not to strike the hoop, but to position his pole so that the hoop, when it ceased to roll, would fall across it. If the hoop fell on any part of a player's pole, he scored one point. To score two points, the hoop had to fall on the butt end of a pole. If a pole pierced the hoop, no score was earned. But if the hoop fell on the pointed end of the pole, the thrower scored three points and won the game.

Certain tribes played variations of the hoop-and-pole game. In the Blackfoot version, a tribesman scored if his pole went through the hoop. In the Arapaho game, a third person rolled the hoop for two players. Pawnee tribesmen hurled darts through rolling hoops, while the Sauk and Fox Indians shot arrows through them.

The Hidatsa Indians of North Dakota used a hoop made of ash wood, crisscrossed with rawhide thongs and woven to make a small hole in the middle—the "heart." When a player speared the heart with his pole, he chased his competitor until he hit him with his hoop. That player rolled it back, shouting, "There is a buffalo charging you!"

STICK-TARGET GAMES

Shuffleboard could very well be a descendent of a stick-and-stone contest held by the Choctaw Indians. A rectangle, roughly forty feet long by three feet wide, was drawn on the ground. The highest scoring area was then indicated by a line drawn across

31

the width of the rectangle, five inches from the end; the lower scoring area extended five inches in front of that. Two players, each equipped with a four-foot-long stick and three round, flat stones, took turns shoving the stones with their sticks toward the scoring areas. The stones were left where they lay until the end of a player's turn, and he sometimes tried to hit one of his stones into another in order to propel the latter into a scoring zone. Stones reaching the lower scoring area counted for one point each, and stones landing in the higher scoring area counted for three points each. The first player to acquire seven points won the round.

Southwestern Indians played a stick-target game called "snakes," a variation of the Indian winter contest, "snow-snakes." The sticks were three-foot-long, polished rods of hard-wood, tapering from three inches in diameter at one end to a point at the other. Some Indians carved their sticks to resemble serpents and made notches in the tail ends for their throwing fingers.

The game was played on any stretch of level ground by any number of competitors. Each balanced his stick on his left hand and placed the forefinger of his right hand against the blunt end of his stick. He then threw it underhand in an attempt to make it skim along the ground and outdistance his rivals' missiles.

The Chippewa tribes held "jumping frog" competitions, using an oval-shaped tipcat ° and a stuffed, buckskin ball tied to a stick by a three-inch cord. The object of the game was to strike either end of the wooden tipcat with the ball attached to the stick and to send the tipcat up in the air. The player who missed was out of the game.

° *see page 64*

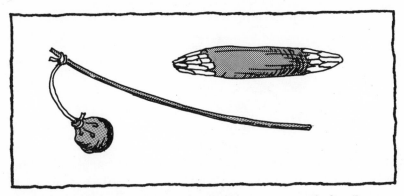

Ginskut was the favorite stick-target game of the Papago Indians of southern Arizona and northern Mexico. The ground was marked with a square. Three of its corners had seven dots each and the fourth corner had a circle of dots, representing the sun. Each player took four two-foot-long sticks and placed them on a stone in the center of the square. Then each in turn struck the sticks with another stone, causing the sticks to fly upward. The stick-thrower scored one point for each stick that fell on any of the corners containing the seven dots. The player who scored the highest number of points, or the player whose stick was the first to land on the corner with the sun, won the game.

The Pomo and Yokuts tribes of California originated a stick-target game in which each player was equipped with a "stick," consisting of a cigar-shaped bundle of reeds, tied together at each end. The players of two teams faced each other across the dividing line of a playing area ten feet wide by twenty feet long. When a signal was given, each player heaved his reed bundle at the shins of one of his opponents, who tried to hop nimbly aside in order to avoid being struck. But if he was unsuccessful, he was disqualified and forfeited his stick. The player who hit him grabbed the forfeited stick and hurled it, and then his own stick, at another opponent. The winning side was the first to disqualify every member of the rival team.

The Hopi Indians held marksmanship contests in which they hurled a type of non-returning boomerang called a "rabbit stick," which they used to kill rabbits and other small game. The object was to see who could strike the greatest number of corncobs tossed in the air by a non-player.

TOP-SPINNING CONTESTS

Top-spinning ° was one of the favorite pastimes of both Indian women and children. The Chinook tribal women of the Pacific Northwest played top-spinning games with disks carved out of ivory or whalebone, with pegs inserted through the disks' centers. Each player twirled the upper half of the peg between the palms of her hands in order to set the top spinning. The player whose top spun the longest, without leaving a circular enclosure drawn on the ground, won the contest.

Iroquois tribeswomen played a whip-top game with carved wooden tops and whips made of several rawhide strips attached to saplings. A small square, with four-inch openings on each side, was marked on the ground. Each player started her top spinning outside the square and then tried to be the first to whip her spinning top through one of the four openings.

° *also see Winter Sports and Games*

◄═5═► WATER SPORTS

Most Indian tribes regarded swimming as a life-saving necessity or an adjunct of warfare, rather than a sport. For the most part, they imitated animals' movements in the water and became expert "dog-paddlers" and underwater swimmers. But the style we know as the Australian crawl was nothing new to many tribesmen—a fact Europeans discovered when a group of North American Indians competed for a silver medal in London in the mid-nineteenth century.

Indian children, with the exception of those who lived in northern Canada, were taught to swim at an early age. The Plains tribes spent much of their time in the water during the late spring and summer months. So did the Indians who inhabited the Pacific Northwest, where the ocean was warmed by the Japanese current.

A desire to increase their speed and expertise in swimming naturally resulted in rivalry between tribal and intertribal swimmers. In addition to underwater and relay swimming races, the Indians developed several forms of aquatic sports, such as log-rolling and canoeing contests.

In the Pacific Northwest, ocean-going canoes were made from hollowed-out trunks of the giant Sequoia trees that grew at the water's edge. The great canoes of the Haida and Tlinglit tribes had high, colorfully decorated and carved prows, and were capable of carrying up to fifty Indians.

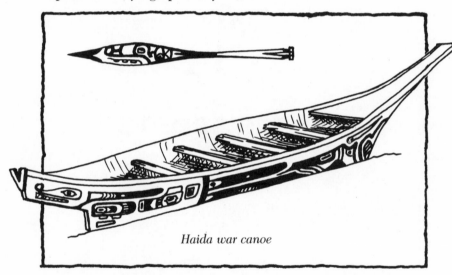

Haida war canoe

On the Atlantic coast, Indian dugouts were simply constructed, smaller craft, with rounded ends. The Seminole, and several other tribes who lived in the Southeast and below the Mexican border, had narrow dugouts with platforms in the sterns for poling. The Plains Indians, who lived near the Missouri River, used circular, tub-shaped bullboats. They were made of willow branches, woven into a hardwood frame, and covered with rawhide. The seams were sealed with tallow and ashes.

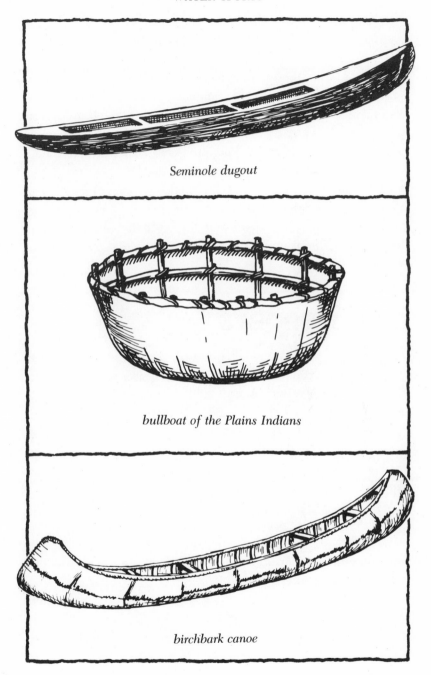

Seminole dugout

bullboat of the Plains Indians

birchbark canoe

Elsewhere, however, the birch-bark canoe dominated the waterways. Early explorers and settlers soon found that Indian bark canoes were far superior to the wooden boats the Europeans had brought with them. The Indian canoes drew very little water, and were swift, maneuverable, and easily repaired. A boat large enough to carry six men and their supplies weighed approximately a hundred pounds, and could easily be lifted on a man's shoulders for portages.

But no matter how the Indians' boats or canoes were shaped, nor which materials were used, the tribes took great pleasure in trying to outdistance each other in the races they held. Over the centuries they kept on improving their craft so as to give them greater speed.

CANOE SPORTS

The Chippewa, who were master canoe-builders, played a game in which each competitor was equipped with a six-foot-long pole, one end of which was padded. Each canoe contained a tilter, who stood at the bow, and a paddler. The object was to dislodge the tilter in the opposing canoe by pushing or punching him with the pole. If a tilter fell in the water, or into his canoe, he was disqualified, and the opposing canoeists became the winners.

Northeastern tribes played a tug-of-war game with their canoes. When two boats were attached by a five-foot rope, the tribesmen in each canoe paddled in opposite directions. The team that pulled the other team past a log, anchored in the water, won the contest.

The Leni-Lenape Indians of Delaware held races in which each contestant paddled his canoe to a turning point. He then overturned the boat and swam back to the starting line, towing it with him.

FLOATING-LOG GAMES

Log-rolling was a popular water sport of many tribes. Two men stood on top of the same log anchored in the water. Each had a balancing pole, a slender twelve-foot-long sapling. He held the smaller end and placed the other end about a foot below the water's surface. At a signal, each player began rolling, slowing, or stopping the log in an attempt to dislodge his competitor.

The Creek Indians of the Southeast vied with one another in a contest in which each man stood on a floating log. The one who could roll it farthest, without falling off, was the winner.

6

WINTER SPORTS AND GAMES

When the temperature plunged, the snow piled high, and the ice-jammed rivers ceased to flow, Indians who lived in the vast northern regions of the continent were often preoccupied with their quest for food. But if a tribe had an ample supply of dried fish, venison, caribou, or other meat on hand, then the long, bleak winter was a time of feasting, sports, and games.

If the weather became too severe, an entire storm-bound village might assemble in a large, communal structure, where they would pass the time by weaving intricate string figures, and by watching or taking part in wrestling matches, dancing, games of chance, and guessing games. But whenever possible, the tribes engaged in a wide range of outdoor sports.

ICE SHINNY

The Indians' shin-bruising version of ice hockey was played in the same manner as shinny.° Two upright logs, serving as goal

° *also see Ball Games*

posts for each team, were placed one-quarter of a mile apart on a frozen river or lake. The puck was a rawhide-covered, round knot of wood, or a sphere carved out of stone. With their curved sticks, the fifty players on each team slammed the puck—and sometimes each other—in an attempt to drive it between their opponents' goal posts. As in shinny, the first team to score seven points won the game.

Ice shinny was also a favorite winter sport of the Sioux, Crow, and Blackfoot tribeswomen of the Plains, who had an impartial method of choosing two teams. Each player put her individually carved shinny stick on a pile. A blindfolded non-player was then asked to pick them up, two at a time, and to place one stick on her right side and the other on her left. In that way she allocated each player to a team.

SNOW-SNAKES

This was a favorite pastime of the Northeastern, Northwestern, and Prairie tribes. A narrow rut was made in the snow by dragging a large tree limb along the surface. Each player had his own "snake," a slender, three-foot-long stick, which he held lengthwise above the rut. Then he took several short, quick steps, and threw his stick along the rut. The winner was the one who was able to slide his stick the farthest.

The Seneca and other clans of the Iroquois tribe played a variation of snow-snakes, called "snow-boats." The fifteen-inch boats were carved out of beechwood in the shape of a canoe. The playing field was a hill with a flat meadow below it. Each player made his own trench—down the hillside and out onto the meadow—by trampling on the snow. When he had poured water into the trench lining and had let it freeze, he dipped his boat in water to give it a slippery coating of ice and slid it down the hill. The owner of the boat that slid the farthest was the winner.

CHUNKEY

The Chippewa are said to have pioneered this sport°, which was played on the ice with a smooth, stone disk and a long pole, crooked at one end. Two men normally played the game. As one contestant rolled a stone disk down a designated course on the ice, both players slid their poles after it. The object was to slide a pole in such a way that the disk, when it stopped rolling, would be caught in the pole's crook. The player who won the round earned the right to roll the disk in the next game.

Chunkey was one of the oldest winter sports of the American Indian. Archaeologists have discovered a number of chunkey stones in prehistoric mound-sites and chunkey yards of ancient Indian villages in the Northeast.

SNOWSHOE AND TOBOGGAN RACING

Snowshoes enabled the Indians to walk on snow without sinking. Although their designs differed considerably, the shoes generally consisted of light frames of hardwood, roughly the shape of large tennis rackets. They were strung with rawhide strips, and attached to the wearer's boots or moccasins behind a central crossbar near the front of each shoe. When caught by a sudden snowstorm, an Indian could quickly improvise an emergency pair of shoes by bending green willow branches and webbing them with strips of bark.

The Khotana tribe of the Far North used snowshoes which were triangular in shape, and another type which were circular. The latter provided wide support in the soft snow, and were easily maneuverable on upland trails. The Cree Indians, farther south in Canada and Montana, used a long, narrow shoe about six feet in length, developed for speed in open country. The Cree

° *also see Dexterity and Marksmanship Games*

and the Chippewa held snowshoe sprints on marked courses that ran up and down hills and along flat ground as well.

Toboggans were used by the northern Indians from Labrador to the Yukon. They were made in various sizes, but all were constructed of smooth, wooden planks, curved upward at the

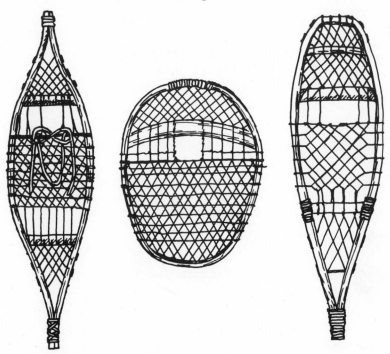

front end in order to slide easily over irregularities in the snow's surface.

Toboggan racing, the forerunner of bobsledding, was an Indian sport of coasting down chutes, which were made by dragging a log down a snowy hillside. The racer steered by shifting his weight or trailing his feet.

"Toboggan swimming" was a race held on a flat surface. Each racer lay on his stomach on his toboggan at a starting line. When a signal was given, he pushed with his hands and feet to the finish line.

Another kind of toboggan race was run by two teams, each

numbering eight tribesmen—one rider and seven pullers. Each of the pullers held onto the belt of the parka of the man in front of him. A deerhide cord, held by the rider, was then looped around the waist of the last man. The first team to finish the 220-yard course, with all racers in position, won the contest.

OTHER WINTER SPORTS

The Penobscot Indian women of the Northeast had their own unique brand of tug-of-war. A stout rope of braided rawhide strips was run through a small hole in a four-foot wall of packed snow, and each team of twelve women tried to pull its rival team members through the wall.

Snowball-rolling was also a Penobscot game. Each player started with a snowball one foot in diameter, which he rolled along a set course. The roller with the biggest snowball at the finish line was the winner.

Ingenious Plains Indians conducted races on sleds, which they constructed of ten buffalo rib-bones, with willow crossbars lashed tightly together with rawhide.

The Nootka and Tlinglit Indians of the Pacific Northwest spun birchwood tops on ice or hard-packed snow. With a quick twist of the wrist, each player started his top and kept it spinning by lashing at it with a willow branch. The object of the game was to see who could spin his top the greatest number of times within a twenty-foot circle of snow in which small trenches had been dug. It required a great amount of practice and skill to whip a top so that it would jump across a trench and still keep spinning after it landed. The winner of each game kept the loser's top.

The Teton Dakota tribe played a top game on river ice with whips and round stones. Two players spun their stones and whipped them together as hard as they could. The one whose stone cracked another's, and continued to spin the longest after the collision, was the winner.

GUESSING GAMES

Guessing games, some of the North American Indians' most popular forms of amusement, fell into three categories: moccasin games; hand games; and stick games.

Simple objects, such as pebbles, peeled twigs, or bone

cylinders, were used in most guessing games. But the equipment used by the Pacific Northwest tribes reflected their outstanding skill as carvers. Their playing sticks were often inlaid with intricate patterns of abalone shell and ivory. On an even more opulent note, Aztec and Toltec guessing-game sticks, unearthed at archaeological sites in Mexico, were carved of jade, turquoise, and other semi-precious stones.

MOCCASIN GAMES

Two teams of two men each played this game on a blanket or an animal hide spread on the ground. When four moccasins were placed in its center, one of the players took four small stones, one of which was marked, and put one in each of the moccasins. While doing this, he tried his best to distract his opponents. He shook the stones in both his hands, sang songs, made funny faces, or performed sleight-of-hand tricks. When all of the stones had been distributed, a player on the other team tried to guess in which moccasin the marked stone was concealed. If he made four correct guesses in a row, he won the game. The score was kept with tally sticks.

The Delaware Indians used six moccasins in their version of the game, and the Navajo tribes used as many as eight. Pima Indians of the Southwest placed a bean into one of four hollow pieces of reed, which they then filled with sand. Players had to guess in which reed the bean had been hidden. The Walapai Indians of northeastern Arizona played the game with a long trench, dug in sandy soil. A player grasped a ball, carved out of yucca root, in his left hand, and then drew it along the bottom of the trench. As he did this, he piled sand over his buried hand with his right hand. When he withdrew both hands, his competitors tried to guess where in the trench the ball was hidden.

When the moccasin game was introduced by the Indians to the early European settlers, the latter used bullets instead of stones. At one point, the game was banned in the Indiana Territory because the settlers had become addicted to it.

HAND GAMES

Each of the four players on two teams tried to guess in which hand a member of the other team had hidden three pebbles. The person holding the stones made many deceptive movements in order to confuse his opponents. He placed his hands above his head or behind his back, and passed—or pretended to pass—the pebbles to one of his confederates. The player who made five correct guesses in a row won the round for his team. If he was able to guess correctly on the first attempt, he became the hider for his team.

The California Indians played a variation of the hand game. One player hid in his hands two small, bone cylinders, one of which was marked with a painted symbol. An opponent then tried to determine which hand held the unmarked cylinder. If he guessed correctly, he kept his competitor's bones; if he was incorrect, he lost his bones to his opponent. Sets of painted gaming bones were prized possessions of the tribe, and were handed down from generation to generation.

STICK GAMES

A favorite Indian guessing game was played with various kinds of sticks. The Haida and Tlinglit Indians, and the Cree tribes of eastern Canada, played a game with a bundle of eighteen four-inch sticks, each carved with a different symbolic design. When a player had divided a bundle into nine sticks each, his opponent had to guess which bundle contained a stick with a particular design painted on it.

When the Cree Indians played the game, they used twenty-five peeled willow twigs, which they grouped into two lots. A player who was able to guess which bundle concealed the even number of sticks won the game.

Another version of the stick game was played by any number of Prairie tribesmen. After a contestant dropped a bundle of fifty willow sticks in a pile on the ground, he then took a long, pointed stick and tried to separate twenty-five sticks from the pile. If he had successfully divided the fifty sticks in half, he scored one point. If not, another player took his place. The first participant to score fifty points was the winner.

8

GAMES OF CHANCE

Indian games of chance were played with many kinds of equipment. In ancient ruins from the Pacific to the Atlantic coasts, and from northern Canada to Panama, archaeologists have found dice in various shapes and sizes: disks made of wood, pottery, bone, and horn; river and sea shells; halved nutshells; fruit pits; and sticks carved out of deer bones, reeds, wood, and animals' teeth. Unlike the six-sided cubes we use today, Indian dice were almost always two-sided objects.

Indian tribesmen usually tossed their dice in a shallow basket or in a wooden cup or bowl. Some Indians placed dice in a basket, tossed them in the air, and caught them in the basket. Others tossed dice by hand, or shook a dice-filled basket and threw the contents on the ground.

Casting dice to see how they fell fascinated North American tribesmen, and they sometimes staked their possessions—arrows, blankets, pipes, and even horses—on the flip of a gaming piece.

But the Indians also had dice games in which skill often outweighed the law of chance. The women of the Kiowa and Wichita tribes, for example, played a game similar in many respects to parcheesi. And long before Cortez began his conquest of Mexico, the Aztec tribes played *patolli*, a recognizable version of backgammon, which later spread as far north as Colorado and the Dakotas.

STICK-DICE GAMES

Indian stick-dice were two-sided pieces of wood, bone, or horn, ranging from three inches to two feet in length. Some sticks had one side painted with a color, or carved with a design, while the other side was unadorned; some sticks were flat on one side and rounded on the reverse; and other sticks were painted a different color on each side. The Arapaho and Hidatsa Indians both painted and carved their stick-dice, which they made out of willow saplings. The Beaver, Sarsi, and Cree tribes of Canada fashioned stick-dice out of elk antlers. The Chippewa, Wyandot, and Ottawa tribes of the Lakes region carved their sticks into elongated bird and animal shapes.

One of the simplest forms of Indian dice games, using only one four-inch stick, was played by two or more tribesmen. The marked side of the stick counted for one point; the unmarked side counted for two. The object was to be the first tosser to reach a score of twenty.

Pugasaing, one of the most widely played Indian stick-dice games, required three sticks, painted red on one side and white on the other. Two teams, consisting of two players each, took turns throwing the dice. The first player shook the sticks in a basket and tossed them on the ground, scoring them as they fell.

Three white sides up counted three points; three red sides up counted two; two reds and one white up counted one point; and two whites and one red counted none. The first side to score over twenty points won the game.

California tribes played a game with four stick-dice, each with a different pattern. Each player tried to be the first to throw in sequence the full set of sticks, with the patterned sides up. The first to reach a score of twelve points won the game. The same game was played with plum or peach stones, each marked on one side with dots numbering from two to twelve.

The Pueblo, Pima, and other tribes of the Southwest played a stick-dice game with a counting board made of stones placed on the ground in a circle. The circle had four divisions of ten places each, with openings at the four points of the compass. According to each player's toss of the dice, he moved a small twig around the circle. The winner was the first player to move his twig around the entire circle and back to its starting place. If a twig landed on a spot occupied by an opponent's twig, the latter had to be returned to its starting point.

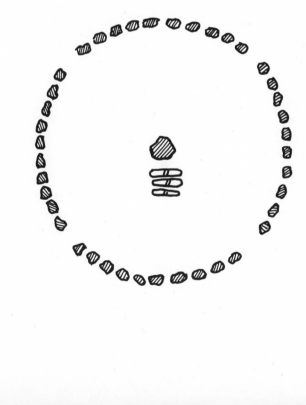

STONE-DICE GAMES

The Nez Percé tribes of central Idaho played a game using four flattened plum stones, painted black on one side and unpainted on the other. Each player was allowed only four tosses. There was only one scoring toss: four black sides up counted four points. A toss of four plain sides up, or any combination of plain or marked sides up, disqualified a player. The first tosser to score twenty points was the winner. A similar game, *Tunkan*, was played by the Sioux Indians, who used painted plum stones.

"Fighting Serpents," an Aztec game reminiscent of backgammon, was played by two contestants. One player had a set of twenty-three plum stones, painted black; the other player had an

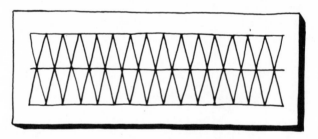

equal quantity of plum stones, painted white. Three parallel lines were drawn on the ground, and these were intersected by forty-nine lines, forming a diamond pattern. The plum stones of each player were then positioned on all the intersections except the three along the middle parallel lines—the two outermost intersections and the one at the center. Each player shook two plum-stone dice, each carved on one side. The first to throw the carved sides up won the chance to start the game. The first player moved one of his stones along a line to any of the three unoccupied points. Then the other player took over. Capturing an opponent's stones, whenever possible, was mandatory—even if a player had a choice of moves. A competitor's stone was captured by jumping over it to an empty point directly beyond it, without changing direction. But once a player had captured his opponent's stone, he was allowed to change his direction. Each time a stone was taken, it was removed from the playing area. If a player was unable to capture another's stone, he could move one of his own along a line in whatever direction he chose. The first player who captured all his opponent's stones was the winner.

Kuntassoo, a forerunner of parcheesi, was a game for four players, originated by Prairie tribeswomen. They used two plum-stone dice, each side of which was carved with dots, numbering from two to five. Four bean counters, each painted a different

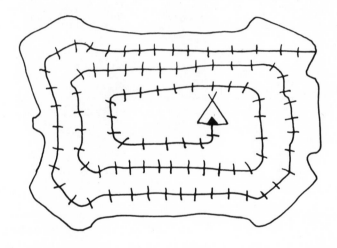

color, were then distributed among the four players. Painted on a rawhide skin was a trail, spiraling inward from a starting point on the border of the hide to a teepee painted on the center of the hide. Little lines, representing streams, bisected the trail at short intervals. The first player placed her counter at the starting point, between the first and second streams. She then tossed the dice on the ground. The dots appearing on their uppermost sides indicated the number of spaces she could move her counter forward. But whenever the dots on the uppermost sides of the dice totalled seven, she was forced to return to the starting point. Each player in turn was allowed a toss of the dice, and the one whose counter was the first to reach the teepee won the game.

HOW TO MAKE INDIAN
GAMING EQUIPMENT

Directions for making replicas of Indian gaming equipment are given in square measures. Tables of metric equivalents and conversions are included at the end of this chapter.

Note: Certain pieces of equipment require a minimal amount of whittling. One of the most effective kinds of whittling tools is a pocketknife with two or more blades of varying sizes. Hold the knife handle with a firm grip and cut away from yourself, pressing down and forward. Always cut with the grain of the wood (Figure 1).

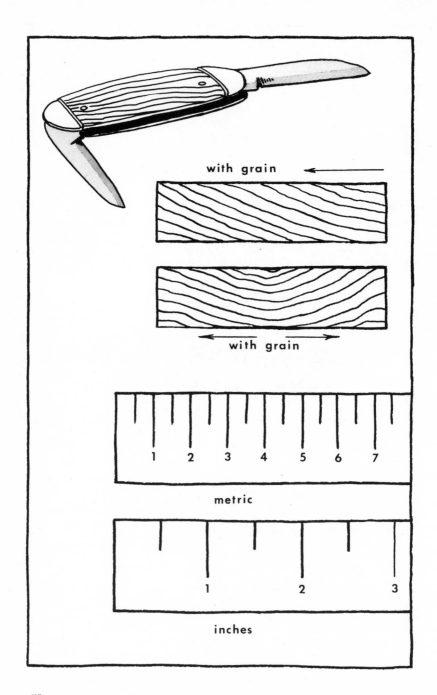

with grain

with grain

metric

inches

INDIAN BALL

(Ball games are described in Chapter 2.)

Materials

12″ square piece of chamois or synthetic leather
linen or heavy-duty thread
large needle
pair of scissors
gravel or other stuffing, such as dried beans or styrofoam

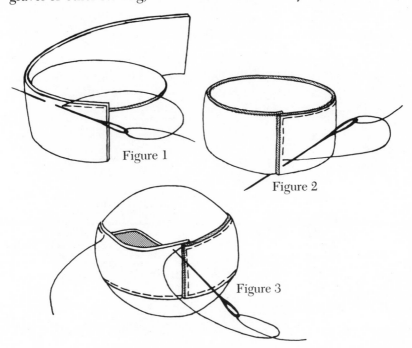

Figure 1

Figure 2

Figure 3

1. Cut two circles, each 2¾″ in diameter, and an 8½″ × 2″ strip of the chamois or other material.
2. Sew one side of one circle to the 8½″ strip, overlapping the

seam (Figure 1). Sew the ends of the strip together.

3. Sew the remaining circle to the strip (Figure 2), but leave a small opening in which to put the gravel or other material. Stuff the ball.

4. Sew up the opening and bind off securely (Figure 3).

Note: The Oto Indians of Oklahoma, and other Prairie tribes, used this kind of ball in their lacrosse games.

IROQUOIS SNOW-SNAKE

(Snow-snake contests are described in Chapter 6.)

Materials

tree branch, approximately 7″ long and 1″ in diameter
two or more feathers (depending on size), preferably 6″ long
small hand drill
white glue
knife
enamel paint and brush (optional)

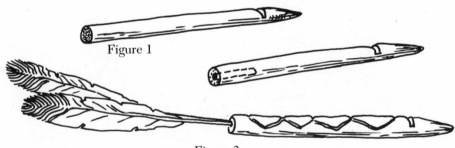

Figure 1

Figure 2

1. Scrape the bark off the branch and whittle one end of it into a point (Figure 1).

2. Drill a small hole, approximately 2″ deep, in the untapered end of the branch. Take as many feathers as the hole will accommodate, apply glue to their quill ends, and insert them in the hole.
3. The snow-snake can be decorated with paint, or carved with a design (Figure 2).

RING-AND-PIN EQUIPMENT

(Ring-and-pin games are described in Chapter 5.)

Materials

corncob or multi-colored ear of Indian corn
twig or wooden dowel, ⅜″ in diameter and approximately 8″
   long
cord
small hand drill
knife
pair of scissors

1. Strip husks and silk from corncob. Trim the larger end.
2. Drill a hole, ⅜″ in diameter and 2½″ deep, in the corncob's largest end.
3. Whittle one end of the twig or dowel to a point. Make a small notch ½″ from the other end.
4. Loop the cord several times around the notched part of the twig and tie securely. Loop the other end of the cord around the smallest end of the corncob and tie securely (Figure 1).

Note: Hold the twig, or "pin," in one hand and toss the corncob upward with the other hand. The object is to thrust the pointed end of the pin into the corncob's hole (Figure 2).

61

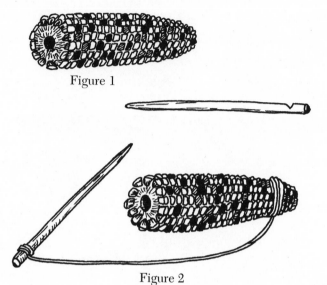

Figure 1

Figure 2

HOOP-AND-POLE

(Hoop-and-pole games are described in Chapter 4.)

Materials

sapling branch, approximately 36″ long
pole or broom handle, 3′ long
three rawhide thongs, each 40″ or longer
knife
pair of scissors

1. Trim the bark from the sapling and taper each of its ends.

2. Bend the sapling into a circle and overlap the tapered ends. Bind with thongs and tie securely (Figure 1).
3. Stretch a rawhide thong across the center of the hoop and tie (Figure 2).
4. Taper each end of the pole or broom handle in order to make it slide smoothly along the ground (Figure 3).

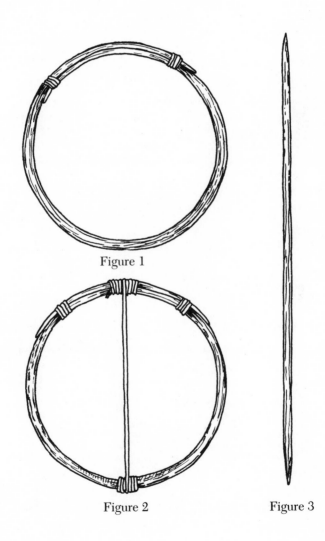

Figure 1

Figure 2

Figure 3

JUMPING FROG

(Rules for playing Jumping Frog are given in Chapter 4.)

Materials

piece of wood, approximately 7″ long and 1½″ in diameter
10″ stick or branch, approximately ⅜″ in diameter
9″ square piece of chamois or synthetic leather
pair of scissors
strong cord, 36″ or longer
large sewing needle
one to two cups of dried split peas or gravel

1. Make a tipcat by whittling each end of the 7″ piece of wood into rounded points (Figure 1).
2. Cut a circle, 8″ in diameter, out of the chamois or synthetic leather.
3. Thread the needle with the cord and sew an even, running stitch around the circle, approximately ⅛″ from the perimeter. Leave the ends of the cord long (Figure 2).

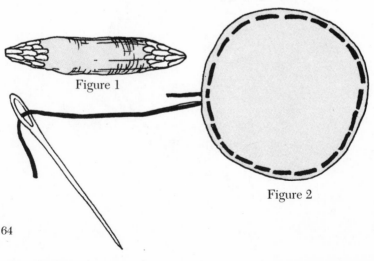

Figure 1

Figure 2

Figure 3

4. Draw the two ends of the cord together to form a cup. Fill the cup with split peas or gravel.
5. Draw the ends of the cord tightly and tie them together, but leave one end of the cord 8" long.
6. Tie the cord to one end of the 10" stick or branch. The cord should measure 4" between the stick and the ball (Figure 3).

KUNTASSOO GAMING EQUIPMENT

(Rules for playing *Kuntassoo* are given in Chapter 8.)

Materials

two clean fruit pits (prune, peach, or plum)
1 yard of white or light-colored felt, 72" wide
four dried lima beans or four small, flat pebbles
small paint brush
tempera or enamel paint (white and three other colors)
waterproof, felt-tipped marker (black)
pair of scissors

1. Paint each of the four dried beans or pebbles a different color.
2. Paint two white dots on one side of one fruit pit, and three

dots on the reverse side. Paint four dots on one side of the
other pit, and five dots on its reverse side

3. Place the felt on a flat surface. If you prefer, you can cut it
into the shape of an animal hide (Figure 1).

4. With a felt-tipped marker, draw a teepee (or an equilateral
triangle 1½″ high) in the center of the felt. Select a starting
point at the outer edge of the felt and draw a line, spiralling
inward to the teepee. Intersect the line with 1″ lines spaced
1½″ apart (Figure 2).

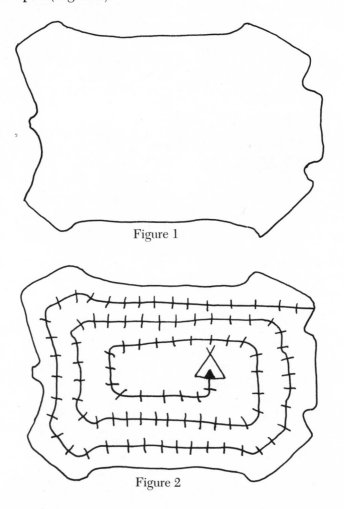

Figure 1

Figure 2

STICK-DICE

(Descriptions of stick-dice games are given in Chapter 8.)

Materials

four sticks, each ½" wide × 4" long, and approximately
⅛" thick
knife
enamel paint (red, white, and black)
small paint brush

1. With a knife, round off the ends of each stick (Figure 1).
2. Paint one side of each of the four sticks red
3. Paint a different design on the other side of each stick (Figure 2).

Figure 1

Figure 2

Materials

three sticks, each ½" wide × 4" long, and approximately ⅛"
 thick
enamel paint (red and white)
small paint brush

1. Paint one side of each stick red, and paint the reverse side of
 each stick white.

Note: Red-and-white stick-dice were used in the game of
 Pugasaing.

HOPI DARTS

(Information about target games is provided in Chapter 4.)
Materials

four small corncobs
four 2" finishing nails
small hammer
hand drill
eight or more feathers (depending on size), each approximately
 4" long
white glue
knife

1. Strip husks and silk from corncobs and scrape off their
 kernels. Cut a section, ½" long, off the largest end of each
 corncob.
2. With a hammer, drive a finishing nail, head first, into the
 narrowest end of each corncob. Make sure the nails are firmly
 in place (Figure 1).

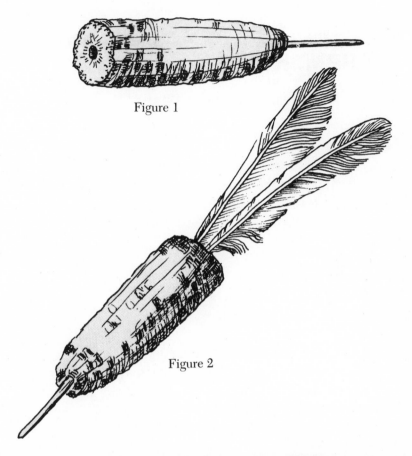

Figure 1

Figure 2

3. Drill a small hole, 2″ deep, in the largest end of each corncob, and insert as many feathers as the hole will accommodate. Apply glue to the quill ends of the feathers, and insert them in the holes of the corncobs (Figure 2).

Note: The darts can be thrown on targets drawn in sand or on the ground, or they can be hurled at rings placed on the ground or suspended by a cord tied to the branch of a tree. (See page 71.)

FIGHTING SERPENTS GAMING EQUIPMENT

(Rules for playing Fighting Serpents are given in Chapter 8.)

Materials
piece of smooth-surfaced wood, 20″ × 8″
two clean fruit pits (prune, peach, or plum)
waterproof, felt-tipped pen or grease pencil
ruler
white paint
small brush
twenty-three dried red beans
twenty-three dried lima beans
clear varnish and brush (optional)

1. Paint one side only of each fruit pit.
2. With a pen or a grease pencil and a ruler, draw three horizontal lines 16″ long and 2″ apart. Mark a dot at 1″ intervals on the top and bottom lines (Figure 1).

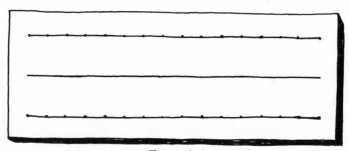

Figure 1

3. Draw a line connecting the first dot on the top line and the second dot on the bottom line. Repeat the process across the length of the line. Do the same in the opposite direction (Figure 2).

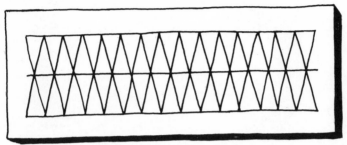

Figure 2

TARGET RING

Materials

enough vines or reeds to make a braided ring, approximately
 3½″ in diameter
pair of scissors
cord of twine

1. Braid three strands of reeds or stripped vines (Figure 1).

Figure 1

2. Coil the braided material into a circle, approximately 3½" in diameter. Overlap ends, bind the cord around them, and tie securely (Figure 2).

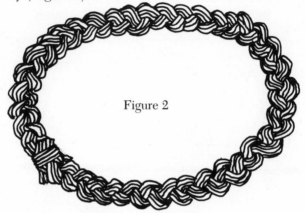

Figure 2

WHIP-TOP EQUIPMENT

(Whip-top games are described in Chapters 4 and 6.)

Materials

6" square piece of cardboard or grocery carton top
small branch or twig, approximately 7" long and ½" in diameter
two small rubber bands
knife
pair of scissors
paint brush
tempera paint or felt-tipped markers (various colors)
sapling branch, approximately 14" long
two rawhide thongs or leather shoelaces, approximately 10" long

1. Cut a circle of cardboard, 5" in diameter, and punch or cut a hole in its center.

2. Decorate the circle with concentric bands in various colors or with designs (Figure 1).
3. Scrape the bark from the 7″ twig and whittle one end into a point.
4. Insert the twig in the cardboard hole so that the pointed end extends 3″ below the cardboard circle; the other end should extend 4″ above it (Figure 2).
5. In order to hold the cardboard circle in place, wind a rubber band tightly around the uppermost part of the twig and slide the band down to the cardboard circle. Repeat the process with the second rubber band and the pointed end of the twig.
6. Strip the sapling of leaves and tie two leather thongs or shoelaces to the tip of the narrowest end (Figure 3).

Note: Set the top spinning by twirling the upper half of the twig between the palms of the hands. The top can be kept spinning by flicking it with the thongs attached to the sapling.

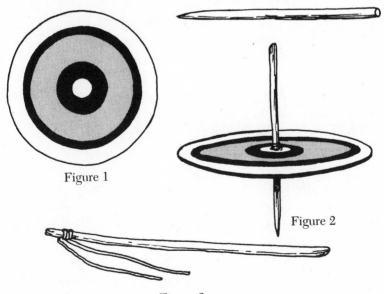

Figure 1

Figure 2

Figure 3

OTO LACROSSE STICK

(Lacrosse is described in Chapter 2.)

Materials

straight tree branch, 44″ long and 1″ in diameter
2 yards of rawhide thongs
small hand drill
pencil
knife
pair of scissors

1. Strip the bark from the branch. Make two pencil marks on the branch—one 8″ from one end, and one 26″ from the end (Figure 1).
2. Whittle both sides of the branch between the pencil marks in order to give the branch a flat surface. The area between the marks should measure approximately ⅜″ thick (Figure 2). Continue to whittle the branch on one side, from the 8″ mark to the end.
3. Measuring from the 8″ mark, make three additional pencil marks—one at 13″, one at 17″, and one at 21″. Drill a small hole through the branch at each mark (Figure 3).
4. Bend the branch to form a loop so that the center hole B is at the top of the loop. Lash the branch with a rawhide thong at the 8″ mark. Tie the thong securely (Figure 4).
5. From the inside of the loop, pull another rawhide thong through hole A. Bring it around the back of the branch and pull it through hole C (Figure 5).
6. Twist the thong around the loop at hole A and tie it securely to the opposite side of the loop, but do not pull the thong taut; the thong should be somewhat slack (Figure 6).

7. Make a knot at the end of a thong. From the inside of the loop, insert the thong in hole B and pull it over the front of the branch. Insert the thong between the twisted thong across the loop and pull it down to the top lashing on the handle. Tie securely (Figure 7).

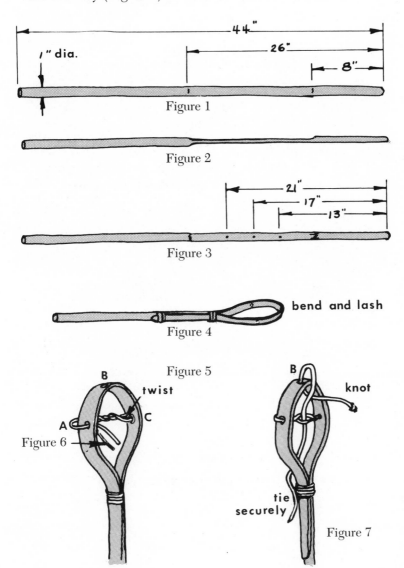

44"

1" dia.

26"

8"

Figure 1

Figure 2

21"

17"

13"

Figure 3

bend and lash

Figure 4

Figure 5

B

twist

C

A

B

knot

Figure 6

tie
securely

Figure 7

COMMON METRIC EQUIVALENTS AND CONVERSIONS

Approximate

1 inch	= 25 millimeters
1 foot	= 0.3 meter
1 yard	= 0.9 meter
1 square inch	= 6.5 square centimeters
1 square foot	= 0.09 square meter
1 square yard	= 0.8 square meter
1 millimeter	= 0.04 inch
1 meter	= 3.3 feet
1 meter	= 1.1 yards
1 square centimeter	= 0.16 square inch

Accurate to Parts Per Million

inches × 25.4°	= millimeters
feet × 0.3048°	= meters
yards × 0.9144°	= meters
square inches × 6.4516°	= square centimeters
square feet × 0.092903	= square meters
square yards × 0.836127	= square meters

° *Exact*

SELECTED BIBLIOGRAPHY

Bleeker, Sonia. *Indians of the Longhouse*. New York: William Morrow & Company, Inc., 1952.

Catlin, George. *Letters and Notes on the Manners, Customs and Conditions of the North American Indians*, 2 vols. New York: Dover Publications, Inc., 1967.

Culin, Stewart. *Games of the North American Indians*. Washington, D.C.: Smithsonian Institution, Twenty-fourth Annual Report of the Bureau of American Ethnology, 1907.

Densmore, Frances. *Chippewa Customs*. Washington D. C.: Smithsonian Institution, Bureau of American Ethnology Bulletin #86, 1929.

Driver, Harold E. *Indians of North America*. Chicago: University of Chicago Press, 1961.

Embree, Edwin R. *Indians of the Americas*. Boston: Houghton Mifflin Company, 1939.

Fletcher, Sydney. *The American Indian*. New York: Grosset & Dunlap, Inc., 1954.

Gallencamp, Charles. *Maya*. New York: David McKay Company, Inc., 1976.

Grinnell, George Bird. *Pawnee, Blackfoot and Cheyenne*. New York: Charles Scribner's Sons, 1961.

Hilger, M. Inez. *Arapaho Childlife and Its Cultural Background*. Washington, D.C.: Smithsonian Institution, Bureau of American Ethnology Bulletin #48, 1952.

Hodge, Frederick Webb. *Handbook of American Indians North of Mexico*. Washington, D.C.: Smithsonian Institution, Bureau of Ethnology Bulletin #30, 2 vols., 1907–1910.

Lowrie, Robert H. *Indians of the Plains*. New York: Natural History Press, 1963.

Morgan, Lewis Henry. *Indian Journals*. Ann Arbor: University of Michigan Press, 1959.

Stern Theodore. *Rubber-ball Games of the Americas*. Seattle: University of Washington Press, 1949.

Stirling, Matthew W. *Indians of the Americas*. Washington, D.C.: National Geographic Society, 1955.

Thompson, Edward. *People of the Serpent*. Boston: Houghton Mifflin Company, 1932.

Vaillant, George C. *The Aztecs of Mexico*. Garden City: Doubleday, Doran & Company, Inc., 1941.

Whiteford, Andrew Hunter. *North American Indian Arts*. New York: Golden Press, 1974.

Wissler, Clark. *Indians of the United States: Four Centuries of Their History and Culture*. New York: Doubleday & Company, Inc., 1966.

INDEX

° Numbers in *italics* indicate pages on which illustrations appear.